the WORLD OF bmx

J.P. PARTLAND & TONY DONALDSON

MBI

To that chrome Redline, an accidental prize, which was stolen before we became intimately acquainted. I hardly knew ye. I wish we had spent more time together.
—*J.P. Partland*

First published in 2003 by MBI Publishing Company, Galtier Plaza, Suite 200, 380 Jackson Street, St. Paul, MN 55101-3885 USA

© J.P. Partland and Tony Donaldson, 2003

MBI Publishing Company books are also available at discounts in bulk quantity for industrial or sales-promotional use. For details write to Special Sales Manager at Motorbooks International Wholesalers & Distributors, Galtier Plaza, Suite 200, 380 Jackson Street, St. Paul, MN 55101-3885 USA

Library of Congress Cataloging-in-Publication Data Available

ISBN 0-7603-1543-4

On the front cover: Feeling gravity's pull at the X Games.

On the frontispiece: Cory "Nasty" Nastazio gives the ladies something to cheer about.

On the title page: A racer finds an inside line and catches some air at the NBL Nationals in Riverside, California.

On the back cover: Rigs are dialed in and awaiting riders at the X Games. Note the low-profile treads used on ramps and at skateparks.

Edited by Dennis Pernu
Designed by Mandy Iverson

Printed in China

contents

acknowledgments

Writing may be a lonely art, but research is extremely social. I thank everyone who took the time to answer my questions. Some of them—the questions—were pretty goofy. Everyone I contacted had an impact, and many are quoted herein.

The world of BMX is tightly knit and leery of outsiders, so thanks to all who let me in and shared their expertise, insight, and, most of all, their passion. These folks include: Adam Stack, Anthony DeRosa, Arizona Race Girl and Friends, Art Absalo, Art Thomason, Bill Curtin, Bob Morales, Brad Hallin, Brendt Barbur, Chris Holmes, Dan Milstein, David Murray, Eddie Fiola, Fuzzy Hall, Gary Sansom, Goldie Leshaun Butler, Gork, Hal Marshman, Heidi Lemmon, Jason Broadaway, Jason Davis, John Pova, Mark Eaton, Mark Losey, Mark Pippin, Mike Daly, Mike Varley, Rob Smart, Ron Mackler, Ron Wilkerson, Shannon Gillette, sKwirl, Steve Olpin, Steve Swope, Taj Mihelich, The Old Man of BMX (Scot Breithaupt), and Van Homan.

— *J.P. Partland*

Ryan Nyquist is one of the top vert and dirt riders plying the craft today. From this angle he looks awfully close to nailing a no-hander lander.

chapter 1

bmx Racing
From busted bikes to breakout action

Head-to-head action from wire to wire is an essential part of the racing thrill.

RIGHT AND ABOVE: In order to get a good gate, racers are moving before the gate completely drops.

If ever there was a sport begging to be named, it was BMX, or bicycle motocross. Since kids first swung their legs over bicycles, they have been riding through dirt, flying over jumps, racing their friends, and trying to outclass one another on tricky courses. But it took the invention of motocross, followed by the drive of some intrepid kids, to turn BMX into its own thing.

Motocross, very simply put, involves riding motorcycles on an unpaved course, whether it's in dirt or mud, through woods or desert. It's about getting away from the road. The motorcycles are raced on technically difficult dirt tracks. After motorcycles took hold in the early part of the twentieth century, flat-track and on-road competitions were next to evolve. Off-road riding, however, took time to develop, but as the technology progressed, so did the popularity of motocross. In the 1960s, the sport boomed, especially among kids. One of the prevalent attitudes among riders was, "If motorcycles can do it, so can bicycles."

A new world of riding was on the map.

Teenage Kicks

Ron Mackler was a teenage employee at Palms Park, a county park in Santa Monica, California. He was running youth programs at Palms when he noticed that kids were riding to the park on their bikes. Mackler was a motocrosser, and he believed he could share the thrills of that sport with the kids at the park.

"We had a big sandbox there," Mackler recalled. "I said, 'Why don't we throw sand on the corners of the sandbox and do some slides?'

"They seemed to have a good time doing it. I would line three or four kids up and they'd go five laps around the sandbox and slide on all the corners. The kids got into it."

"Then, I ran into a guy with a construction business," Mackler continued. "There was another guy named Dave Donovan, who was good with kids, so we got this guy and permission from the parks department to put this track together."

The first bump after the start shoots these riders in the air, giving them enough speed and hang time to clear the second bump without hitting the ground.

The first race at Palms Park was held on July 10, 1969. All the basic ingredients were there: uphill, downhill, berms, jumps, turns, and a flashlight for the starting light. Once word got out, kids came from all over, with some parents driving as long as two hours to get their kids in on the Thursday night action. Some early BMX greats, including Tinker Juarez, Perry Kramer, and Stu Thomsen, came out of those early days at Palms. Mackler ran races at Palms Park for the next 15 years.

Scot Breithaupt was a sponsored, motocross racer around the time Mackler created the course at Palms Park. Only 13 years old, Breithaupt wanted to create a practice course where he could use his bicycle to hone his off-road motorcycle skills. So in 1970, the Long Beach, California, native built a loop in a semi-abandoned space known as Bum's Park—in reference to the homeless people who hung out there—and rode the loop with his friends. In order to make the informal practice sessions "real" races, though, Breithaupt needed a sanctioning body, so he turned the home-field moniker into an acronym and created BUMS, the Bicycle United Motocross Society.

Palms Park and BUMS jumpstarted the new sport. Mackler wanted things to remain accessible and interesting, so he kept the Palms Park fees low: $5 for 10 weeks, with each session featuring up to four hours of racing. He gave out as many certificates, plaques, and trophies as he could and awarded the largest trophy for sportsmanship. If kids couldn't pony up the cash, Mackler let them work it off at the park. He also changed his track around as often as possible and held wheelie and jump contests, or whatever it took to keep the scene hopping.

While Mackler was keeping things as simple as possible, Breithaupt was creating a league with a scoring system,

Riders accelerate through a downhill portion of the course at the Sea Otter NBL Nationals at Manzanita Park in Prunedale, California.

rules, and champions. Breithaupt was both an excellent racer and burgeoning entrepreneur. He convinced 35 kids paying a quarter each at the first BUMS-sanctioned race to give his scene a try, and gave them trophies he had won racing motocross. The second race drew 150 contestants. As the track's popularity grew, Breithaupt helped build others, and by 1974, he had eight tracks, where BMX pioneers like Harry Leary learned the sport.

The origins of the term "BMX," however, remain somewhat of a mystery. Both Breithaupt and Mackler claim credit. There is evidence that the sport was at one time called "pedal cross," but Mackler maintains he called it BMX from the start. Breithaupt says he used the term to explain the sport to national magazines. Some give credit to Elaine Holt, the publisher of *Bicycle Motocross News*, created in 1974.

A rider maintains control through a tight turn, although the front wheel's lack of contact with the ground isn't a good sign. Still, the rider has kept his left foot on the pedal, which indicates that he thinks it's best to pedal through the turn.

LEFT: Proper timing of jumps, like this one in Las Vegas, is critical to racing success.

RIGHT: A rider sets up for a solo turn in Riverside, California. A good line is key in BMX, as in any sort of racing.

Gearing Up for BMX

In the early days, there weren't BMX bikes, only the basic kid ride of the day—Schwinn Sting-Rays and knock-offs from Huffy, Murray, and Sears. Banana seats, sissy bars, tires without knobs, coaster brakes—as long as it had two wheels, cranks, pedals, and a chain, the bike was ready. Or was it?

Most of the bikes featured the classic cantilevered frame that the Schwinn Sting-Ray made famous. Soon, some racers were cutting off the seemingly unnecessary frame tubes that extended forward from the seat tube. These modified frames were lighter but considerably weaker. Often, they failed, though even unmodified frames of the day were relatively weak and couldn't take the pounding. Other racers raised the bottom-bracket height by cutting out some of the seat tube and installing a second bottom-bracket shell. Still others preferred their sisters' bikes, because frames designed for girls made it easier to pull off the funky tricks that were already developing.

Some early racers went for style and practicality by adding equipment like motocross handlebars. The difficulty here, however, was that motocross bars required a shim to fit snugly in the stems. Breithaupt made extra money by selling motocross handlebars, grips, number plates, and other equipment to kids.

The racer in front dictates the pace, both in the air and on the ground.

When Mackler approached a local bike shop and asked for prizes, the employees hooted him out of the place for helping kids destroy bikes. He still chuckles thinking about it. "But when things started selling, they changed their tune real fast," Mackler said.

As the tracks gained credibility through word of mouth, the bike companies began to take notice. BMX's biggest boost, however, came from the motocross movie *On Any Sunday*. Released in 1971, the documentary highlighted the relatively unknown sport of kids racing bikes on dirt tracks. The BMX scenes were short, but they were enough to stir the pot.

Soon after, a number of companies popped up and began to sell BMX gear to kids. While some motorcycle companies got in on the action, more often than not, parents and kids who were already involved in the sport formed the new companies in response to the growing needs they saw. Practical parts like fenders, grips, and handlebars became available, as did accessories like fake gas tanks. The big breakthrough, however, came in 1973 when a new company called Redline introduced a chrome-molybdenum (chro-moly, chrome-moly, or cro-mo) steel frame and unicrown fork that were purpose-built for BMX. The Redline was built by a motorcycle-frame maker, Linn Kasten, and had a higher bottom bracket than Sting-Ray–style bikes, as well as stronger frame tubes, a small saddle, a hand brake, and motocross handlebars.

Because the motorcycle–BMX connection was undeniable, Yamaha decided to get involved in a big way. The company was already well known for motocross, so BMX seemed a natural. In 1974, the company sponsored the Yamaha Gold Cup. Sixteen thousand spectators showed up at the Los Angeles Coliseum for the finals of the three-race series, which was even covered by *Sports Illustrated*. The event's promoter was none other than Scot Breithaupt, who also won the race but was disqualified for being a month too old. After the DQ, Scot became forever known as the "Old Man," or OM, of BMX.

Yamaha used the Gold Cup to promote its BMX bike, a new model with 20-inch wheels and front and rear suspension. Kawasaki followed suit with a suspension BMX bike. Suspension frames were an idea ahead of the time for the nascent sport of mountain biking, but rigid frames

Elbow-to-elbow action is thrilling. Occasionally, the riders get too close and a crash occurs. Take a look at the far right of these pictures. Bam! When one rider biffs, it often creates a chain reaction, taking out whoever is behind and even alongside him or her.

were better for BMX. Both Yamaha and Kawasaki eventually lost the design war to Redline and other garage inventors who began building brands like GT (Gary Turner) and Diamond Back (now Diamondback). Schwinn and Huffy both followed the upstarts, but it took a long time for them to succeed. Breithaupt was in on the bike action as well. In 1976, he debuted an aluminum frame and headed up SE racing, a BMX parts company.

Sailing low over a jump. Oftentimes the best way to maximize speed is to minimize airtime.

Getting Real

Crowds inevitably spawn organizations, and those organizations help regulate and grow a sport. BMX is no exception. In 1973, Ernie Alexander founded the National Bicycle Association (NBA) in California. George Esser formed the National Bicycle League (NBL) the following year in Florida, and in 1977, the American Bicycle Association (ABA) was chartered in Arizona. BUMS faded away. For the rest, it was off to the races.

The big advantage of sanctioning bodies is that they can bring racing communities together. Sure, they impose rules and regulations, but they also provide means of comparing competition in several regions and of determining regional and national champions. The most basic goal of every racer, though, is earning a lower number, which indicates relative rank and provides an incentive every time a rider climbs aboard his or her ride.

The NBA faded away in the late 1970s. The ABA is today larger than the NBL and has more than 60,000 members and about 300 tracks in the United States and Canada. The NBL has over 40,000 members and around 150 tracks in the United States and Puerto Rico. While the NBL is smaller than the ABA, in 1993 it became the only BMX-sanctioning body in the United States that was affiliated with the Union Cycliste International (UCI), the world governing body of bicycle racing. It is hoped that the move, together with the NBL's 1997 membership in USA Cycling, will one day provide a springboard for BMX to get into the Olympics.

Both the ABA and NBL tout that they serve racers from as young as four years of age to as old as 64. Both have three categories per age class. Both have girls' divisions, pro divisions, open races, and classes for both traditional BMX bikes (wheels 20 inches in diameter) and cruisers. This second category, for bicycles with wheels 24 inches and larger, came about in the late 1970s as the first generation of BMX whiz kids became adults. Both the ABA and NBL also tell prospective members that they are the more popular and vital organization.

For most folks, however, the difference is all about location. As Bob Tedesco, managing director of the NBL explained, "People just want to ride their bicycles. If there is an NBL track, they will go there. They're (ABA) stronger in the West. We're stronger in the East. People will go to the closest facility." Both the ABA and NBL offer 30-day trial memberships and have membership magazines.

In terms of clothes and equipment, each organization asks the same things of competitors: long-sleeved shirts, long pants, soft-soled and close-toed shoes, and helmet

Big air with a bit of flair isn't exclusive to vert and dirt riding.

(preferably full-face or with a mouth guard). In addition, each bicycle needs to have at least 20-inch wheels and pads on the handlebar, over the stem, and on the top tube. Reflectors and kickstands must be removed, and a number plate must be affixed. Many tracks loan out helmets and number plates to first-timers.

BMX races are intense bursts of energy and action over courses anywhere from 800 to 1,200 feet in length and usually take less than 45 seconds to complete. Since going full-throttle on a technical course with several others can be intimidating, most tracks schedule practice sessions in addition to race days.

The races themselves are fairly straightforward. The starting gate drops, a wide and downhill drop leads into a turn, and the track narrows, throwing all sorts of difficulties in the riders' faces. The finishes are relatively straight and free of obstacles, which gives everyone a decent shot of sprinting through. Keeping a cool head while sliding, skidding, jumping, and pedaling furiously is key.

Today's BMX tracks include features first made popular in motocross: starting gates, turns, berms, and jumps. The early tracks were much different than those of today. Some were largely uphill, others almost entirely downhill. In most cases, they were very long, often taking more than a

minute to complete. As the sport evolved, so did the tracks, which became shorter so kids could go around them quicker, allowing participants to race multiple times in a single afternoon or evening.

The motos, or heats, are qualifying rounds that determine which riders make the "main," which can either be a single final event or, if there are enough racers, can include semifinals and even quarterfinals. Form dictates that there are three motos before the main, with up to eight riders in each moto. Depending on the size of the field and whether it's an ABA- or NBL-sanctioned event, riders advance either by winning or placing. If there are quarterfinals or semifinals, half of the riders advance. In the main, it's one event for all the marbles.

While a race day or night comprises anywhere from a few to several races, the event is only one in a long season that can last much of the year—some tracks are open year-round. Whether accumulating victories or points, the idea is to work toward the right to have the top-dog number-one on your plate. It's a goal that keeps people training, practicing, racing, racing, and racing some more.

One of the great things about BMX is that just about anyone can do it—boys, girls, grown-ups, and geezers. "Kids who are four years old and men in their sixties are competing," says Anthony DeRosa, director of Central Jersey BMX. The classes, depending on the track and turnout, can be as narrow as "six-year-old novice girls," for example, or as wide as "16 and over open."

The rear end of a BMX bike. The fork ends, or "dropout," hold the axle, which runs through the wheel. The chain rests on a freewheel cog attached to the wheel. The wheel, if you look carefully, uses two different spoking patterns for the right and left side.

A mountain bike shoe and clipless pedal on a BMX race bike. At one time, this was a rare sighting at the races, but now it's common. Mountain bike technology is filtering into BMX, where once it was vice versa.

RIGHT: One "price" of success is signing autographs. In most cases, those doing the signing were once doing the seeking.

Grab a Bike and Go

It's easy to get started in BMX racing. Bikes have come a long way, but even the early bikes offered by Redline, for example, still fit in easily at the local track. In some ways, they're even hot properties, with the retro kick in full gear.

The basic BMX bike is a single-speed rig with a rear brake, small saddle, and high handlebars. Almost anyone either has such a bike or can easily get his or her hands on one. Getting a *good* bike might take a little more work, though.

The heart of any bicycle is the frame. In the early days, chro-moly steel was the ticket. Today, while steel is still plenty real, the frame material of choice is usually aluminum. Aluminum's big advantage is that it's lighter than steel. What makes any bike perform, though, are the dimensions of the frame tubes. The head angle on most BMX frames is around 74 degrees, while racing bikes often have top tubes around 21 inches in length and seat-tube angles of 73 degrees. The chainstays are usually in the 16- to 17-inch range. These dimensions make the bike handle smoothly at high speeds. The bottom-bracket height is usually 12 inches to allow for long cranks and fairly extreme turning while pedaling.

Lately, BMX bikes have taken pages out of the books of their road and mountain bike cousins. This shouldn't be a surprise, since the upstart BMX bike builders of the 1970s are now big companies that produce road *and* mountain bikes, as well as BMX offerings. The hubs on the wheels of a BMX bike, for example, usually have 32 or 36 holes that lead to double-walled aluminum rims. The cranksets are 180 millimeters long and of a three-piece design. The chainring on the crank of a 20-inch bike usually has 44 teeth and is paired with a 16-tooth cog on the rear hub to yield 4.1 meters of development, or the distance a bicycle travels in one revolution of the cranks.

The sophisticated elements don't end there. The brake on a BMX bike is no longer a side-pull, but rather of the powerful V-brake type developed from mountain bike designs. The saddle is usually of the narrow road-racing variety, and pedals are frequently the clipless bindings pioneered by mountain bikers in the early 1990s. The old sharp-tooth platforms still have adherents, but are today losing ground. While road bike design and construction is also coming to BMX in the way of carbon-fiber forks, the classic unicrown pioneered in the early days still has plenty of disciples.

One part of a BMX bike that has remained relatively unchanged over the years is the four-bolt stem, which attaches to the motocross-style handlebars and gives 7 to 8 inches of rise. Most bars are 26 to 27 inches wide.

Cruisers are simply bigger BMX brothers designed to do the same things and to go the same places as the more common and popular 20-inch bikes. Frame geometry is similar. Parts are similar. The chainring teeth are usually dropped down to 39 or 42 on the front with an 18-tooth cog on the rear, yielding 4.5 meters of development. In keeping with tradition, the handlebars usually have a smaller rise, more in the 4- to 5-inch range.

In the end, though, the bike is just a platform. It's the rider, with both fitness and skill, who makes the bike do the amazing things that it does. A moto that lasts less than a minute is really a distilled thrill that can last a lifetime.

The sprint to the finish is usually a colorful flash of riders and bikes.

chapter 2

FLATLAND
FREESTYLIN' bmX TRICKS

This classic flatland move—a switch-footed karl cruiser—says it all.
Impressive skills mean little if not accompanied by an effortless style.

Nashville skyline. Martti Kouppa, a pro flatlander from Helsinki, Finland, works his kickflip with Nashville, Tennessee, in the background. True, flatlanders don't get nearly as much air as their vert and dirt compadres, but they occasionally dump, as the bacon on Martti's knees and shins will attest.

Racing may have been the first BMX discipline, but flatland kicked off the BMX rebellion. Flatland was and still is emphatically *not* racing.

Freestyle, as a descriptive term for flatland riding, came about in the late 1970s, and the few and far between who use the word now are generally old-schoolers or riders who first put down their BMX roots in that era. In short, what was once freestyle is now broken up into several disciplines.

The Birth of Freestyle

Freestyle began as something to do between motos, a way to entertain oneself and friends while waiting to race. It was also a low-key way to practice for the races—working on wheelies, jumping curbs, and figuring out how to brake hard and not crash. Bob Morales, the creator of Dyno Bikes and the American Freestyle Association (AFA), and current proprietor of Morales Bikes was there for some of the earliest trick sessions. He says the freestyle scene started, in part, because the guys doing tricks weren't fast enough on the track. "We were all BMX racers who sucked at racing BMX and didn't like the fact that it was all about winning. Ironically, it became a competition. The original spirit of freestyle was riding your bike and showing off."

While Morales learned from Bob Haro and R.L. Osborn, considered by many to be the pioneers of freestyle, he believes the fire was flinted by the documentary film *On Any Sunday*. "*On Any Sunday,* when Malcolm Smith rode up a tree (on a motorcycle), then rode down backwards, and then rode away," Morales recalled "that right there was the spark that started freestyle." Morales and his friends dreamed of pulling off stunts that cool.

continued on page 34

NEXT: In flatland riding, the bike spends most of its time balanced on one point—a wheel, as demonstrated by this move, a.k.a. the "hitchhiker."

Trevor Meyer works what appears to be an elephant glide.

An X Games rider executes a pinky squeak.

Originally from San Diego, Haro moved in with the Osborn family in Torrance, California, to work for R.L.'s dad, Bob. The Osborns, with Haro as staff artist, started the first glossy BMX magazine, *BMX Action,* the first issue of which was datelined December 1976/January 1977. Working part-time as a journalist in between his days as a fireman, Bob Osborn had been covering the races for the two-fold newspaper *Bicycle Motocross News*. Morales and R.L. Osborn went to the races together and rode when not at the track, when Haro started showing them some tricks in the Osborn driveway. "Haro had a friend in San Diego who was doing stunts like standing on the bike and riding it down the street. Bob had brought those tricks up to us. It kind of gave us something to do in between motos," Morales said. "The first tricks I remember were Bob Haro doing tricks in front of the Osborn house—doing curb endos—then he'd stand on the frame and ride down the street."

The cool tricks and other stuff the guys were working on to impress their friends were the perfect subject for a photographer. R.L.'s sister, Windy, took many of the early freestyle photographs that ended up in *BMX Action*. Suddenly, the media was tying together a growing phenomenon that was being done in similar ways in more and more places. A mag like *BMX Action* was the best way to get information out relatively quickly to the BMX world—the sport wasn't being covered on TV or in newspapers, and the Internet was almost two decades away. Windy Osborn's shots were cool, and readers tried to figure out how the guys got their bikes in such crazy positions.

The photographs were inspiring. With a little time and plenty of practice, most readers thought they could replicate the tricks. Also, there was a practical side to the tricks: they could be done anywhere. Racing was still pretty new, and very few enthusiasts lived in close proximity to a track. Most kids who owned the still relatively new BMX bikes now being manufactured never even hit a track but instead spent most of their time cruising their neighborhoods. Being able to emulate the stars of *BMX Action* was possi-

bly even better than racing. Besides, there was no winner—anyone who could impress somebody was a winner.

Jason Davis, editor of www.notfreestylin.com, remembers his roots: "Freestyle allowed you to find your own way. I enjoyed catching the air in front of everyone much more (than racing). About that time, I was amazed by the riding I would see in the magazines of guys like Bob Haro, Bob Morales, and Tinker Juarez."

Morales pins Haro with coining the name "freestyle," something Haro had taken from skateboarding. Some of the early freestyle BMX moves had parallels in skateboarding, and Davis believes that skating had a strong influence on freestyle. "Skateboarding is that cool cousin you wanted to be just like. We [BMX] have done almost everything 7 to 10 years after skating did."

Skateparks, places where kids could ride the still relatively new creation known as the skateboard, started popping up in California in the 1970s. Skaters, as well as BMXers, had already been riding in empty swimming pools by the time skateparks arrived on the scene. Skaters also played on ramps, half-pipes, and quarter-pipes, as did cyclists. So both skaters and cyclists did tricks, and since the bike tricks seemed to follow freestyle skateboarding, "freestyle" BMX it was.

BMX Action saw a good thing and created the *BMX Action* Trick Team, a squad of freestylin' BMXers who put on shows, promoted *BMX Action,* and did photo sessions that ended up in the magazine. It made business sense, too, because freestyle made BMX more diverse—some even argue freestyle is visually more interesting than racing. Haro and R.L. Osborn were the heart of the first team. Haro eventually left, started his own bike company, and formed the Haro Freestyle Team.

RIGHT: Trevor Meyer goes backyard, walking his bike by standing on a rear peg and scuffing the rear tire.

LEFT: It only looks fast; a variation on the front wheelie seat grab at the X Games.

The Inevitable Competition Scene

With teams doing demos and riders hanging out and trying to figure out their own tricks and emulate those featured in *BMX Action*, it was inevitable that someone would develop a freestyle competition. It was Morales, the anti-competitive guy, who, in 1982, at the age of 18, started the Amateur Skate Park Association to promote freestyle BMX contests. By 1984, the group morphed into the American Freestyle Association (AFA), with competitions featuring both trick—by now referred to as "flatland"—and ramp, or vert, divisions. The sport was so new and small that everyone did everything.

With sanctioned competitions, interest in freestyle grew, just as racing had grown under the auspices of BUMS and later the ABA and NBL. Any company that built bikes for BMX racing also had to build bikes for freestyle and sponsor a demo team to promote the product. *BMX Action* decided that freestyle was big enough to warrant its own mag, so they created *Freestylin'*.

Mainstream media was also catching the wave. Freestyle started appearing in ads and commercials and hit the big time as the plot device for the movie *Rad*, which came out in 1986 and brought the scene to big screens across America. The story is a typical one—that of an unknown, underground figure who comes from nowhere to beat the best factory pros at a BMX race. He gets the girl, too. What made the movie special were scenes featuring some of the best freestyle riders of the day.

Then, around 1989, the bottom fell out of the freestyle world. People suddenly stopped buying bikes, bike companies dropped their teams, venues started charging a lot more for space, and the freestyle world—the side that was visible to the public, anyway—disappeared. Morales first scaled back the AFA and then shelved it in 1990.

A duel in the sun. X Gamers take on a flatland comp.

Everything starts with the basics. The key to rider growth is building, progressing from the known to the unknown. Here, a rider works the basics at the X Games. As he links each move to the next, a run is born.

Back Underground

In reality, though, flatland didn't disappear, it just moved underground. There were still riders out in parking lots, driveways, and streets, doing their thing and letting their passion for riding and discovery fuel them. Just as the AFA was starting its downhill slide, *Dorkin' in York* hit the scene in May 1988. *Dorkin'* was a homemade video created by a bunch of teens who rented a video camera and shot themselves doing flatland tricks in York, Pennsylvania.

They edited the video, added some music, and sold the final product for $10 a pop. They used two VCRs to make copies. Videos were better than stills of moves published in magazines—the setups, execution, and recoveries could all be seen in uninterrupted sequence, making the tricks both more impressive and easier to understand.

The director of *Dorkin'*, Mark Eaton, and his riding buddies, the Plywood Hoods, started shooting the video in 1981. "We'd just shoot footage so we could watch our-

Trevor Meyer shows off one of an endless number of freestyle variations based on the front wheelie.

Chad DeGroot has his bike in a hannah position—straight up and down, his head out front—while working a bar spin.

selves," he recalls. "Kind of a way to see what we were doing wrong." The Hoods were a homegrown freestyle team and also thought they'd use the video to get out the word on their skills. "We rented a video camera, shot a couple of days. We put together a low-budget video, like a video 'zine. The content of the video was the main importance."

Inspired by skate videos like the legendary *Search for the Animal Chin*, the video showed some cool stuff that no one had seen before. *Dorkin*'s top dog was Kevin Jones, who became a star of the underground flatland movement. Today, Jones is viewed by many as the Father of Flatland.

Shortly thereafter, Eddie Roman's *Aggro Riding and Kung Fu Fighting* hit the scene. Video became the way word got out. Riders went to shops, combed the back of magazines for video ads, and scammed copies from their friends. The videos had to be seen to be believed. It was like having a demo invade your house, only you could watch the video demo over and over again, in slow-mo and freeze-frame.

Soon, flatland began its re-ascension, and video was part of the reason. Entire businesses were created to sell videos. In fact, Eaton made a career of the videos, culminating his work with *Dorkin' in York 10*, which highlighted 10 years of making videos. Pro flatlander Art Thomason, of Hoffman Bikes, sees the videos as a great thing. "Videos are great for flatland. Videos are the only way to see the latest, most difficult tricks. Contests are cool, too, but people usually stick to tricks they know they can pull off."

Still, flatland will probably never get the notoriety of other BMX disciplines. Thomason believes that "the lack of flatland coverage stems back to the fact that many people want to see big air or crashes. I think if people took the time to understand flatland, it would be really popular. I mean, ice skating is one of the most popular Olympic sports, and flatland is a lot cooler than that."

RIGHT: DeGroot in mid-tailwhip.

The comparison to figure skating doesn't exactly show the rebellious side of flatland, but it does allude to its difficulty. Eaton also sees the comparison to figure skating, but adds break dancing to the mix—the Plywood Hoods were also break dancers, performing under the name the Cardboard Lords. In both flatland and break dancing, balance is key and not something people pick up overnight. "Any good flatlander has been in it for a long time," Eaton explains. "They're just eccentric. Not many people have the willpower or determination to do it."

Flatland Bikes

Originally, freestyle bikes and BMX racing bikes were one in the same, because there was little demand for a specialized ride. Even with demand, it takes time to figure out what a new sport needs in the way of good equipment. For starters, a front brake was necessary to allow freestylers to stand on their front wheel. Maybe the rider jammed as much air as he could into the tires, because tires with high pressure roll better and ride more predictably than tires with low pressure. Maybe the seat was lowered as far as it could go, but that was the limit of the changes.

One of the first freestyle-specific parts was the Potts modification. In 1984, Steve Potts was a mountain bike designer whose brother-in-law was a flatlander. Potts removed a stem bolt from his brother-in-law's bike, brought it to a machine shop, and drilled a hole through its length wide enough to accommodate the brake cable. The front brake cable was then routed through the modified

continued on page 46

An elephant glide variation. Freestyle moves are so precise that a slight variation can make balance completely different. Because of these differences, flatlanders usually rename the move. The jargon may be difficult to keep up with, but the riding is amazing to watch.

Jaw-dropping tricks are part of the excitement of the X Games. "Howdhedothat?" is the desired reaction. From the improbable one moment to the near impossible just moments later, the progression keeps things exciting for everyone involved.

BELOW: Effraim Catlow performs a hannah variation.

A Torker freestyle bike. Note the rear brake hidden on the chainstays, the pegs, the flat-top tubes for standing, the Odyssey Gyro on the headset, and the brake cable running through the steerer tube.

stem bolt, down through the steer tube, and out the bottom before joining up with the front brake. This minimized the risk of brake cables getting in the way of the turning handlebars. However, there was still the rear brake to deal with.

A year later came the ACS Rotor, a device that attaches to the headset and the rear brake lever, allowing the rear brake to be activated without kinking the cable around the bars or any frame tubes. Riders could now turn their han-

dlebars a full 360 degrees without getting them twisted up in cables. A year after that, the Odyssey Gyro came out.

For riding asphalt and cement, flatlanders didn't need knobby tires that gripped dirt. In fact, knobs are a detriment—they deform under pressure and add rolling resistance. A lightly treaded street tire pumped up to over 100 psi became preferable.

It wasn't long before pegs that screw on to the ends of wheel axles, and on which the rider can stand, became must-have items for freestyle bikes. Most early flatlanders put four on their bike. Some tried building "standers" for their bikes, flat platforms that could be flipped up or down depending on whether the rider planned to use them, but they didn't work out. Mag wheels became another necessity, as they not only seemed stronger, but also provided more space for one's feet. The "cool" factor was pretty high, too.

Haro was the first manufacturer to come out with a freestyle-specific bike, but, really, any BMX bike was enough to start. A specific bike just made moves easier.

As time went on, rider input brought on even more changes that further separated BMX racing bikes from flatland bikes. Some of the input came as factory team riders told their bosses what they needed. The rest came about when riders who couldn't get the bikes they wanted formed their own companies and endeavored to build better bikes on their own.

Oversized pegs are easy to stand on, and radial-spoked front wheels are built to withstand abuse.

Flatland bikes have frame tubes shaped for standing on. Extra curves or flattened sections give more foot room. In 1982, Haro first came out with a twin-top tube design, the Freestyler that made for easy standing. Flatland bikes also have steeper head angles to make them handle better at low speeds and allow the rider to more easily spin the bars and ride them at 180 degrees from their normal position. The flatland bike is also shorter at the top tube and rear end, because bringing the wheels closer together makes it easier to use shifting body weight to perform tricks. With a shorter wheelbase—the distance from the front axle to the rear axle—wheelies are easier. Having the bike shorter from front to rear also makes it easier to climb around it while doing tricks.

In the early days, the weight of freestyle bikes increased, as riders broke frames and parts at an alarming rate. As freestyle went in different directions, though, the need for a sturdy flatland ride wasn't as great as it was for street or vert riders.

Today, the weight of freestyle bikes is dropping rather dramatically. While 4130 chro-moly steel tubing is still very popular because it is cheap, reasonably light, and easy to work with, designers are getting smarter and minimizing the over-building of frames. Double-butted tubes, for years common on road and mountain bikes, shave weight and put enough metal at the joints to keep the bike strong. Other component technology has improved as well, reducing the weight of other parts. Aluminum rims have been redesigned to be stronger while maintaining relatively low weights. At one time, 48 spokes per wheel were common, but now it's back down to a lighter 36. Mags were retired as it became apparent the new rim and spoke designs were just as strong and lighter.

Overall, the flatland bike is small and easy to maneuver. It has to be. Amazingly, today the thing to do among the coolest flatlanders is to ride brakeless. Crazy hard, impossible for beginners, but, in line with the goal of many flatlanders, it's taking the concept to another level.

Trevor Meyer scuffs his way to a win at the Burning Bike Festival in Phoenix, Arizona. Scuffing, using a foot to move the wheel, is a great way to control speed when the brakes aren't handy.

chapter 3

VERT/DIRT
blue skies and
spectacular tries

Cory Nastazio pulls some no-footed air, in this case a Superman seat grab.
Knowing "Nasty," the landing was butter.

Dave Mirra, the X Games' winningest rider, grinds the coping on this ice pick—rear peg on the lip, front wheel in the air.

Using physics to conquer gravity is an old story, but it's one that BMXers put their own twists to and created their own riff. Vert and dirt jumping have their roots in the earliest days of BMX, but it took a while for them to evolve into creatures of their own.

At its most basic, fundamental beginning, skying started with motocross. MXers had jumps, so BMX racers had to have jumps, too. Since there were jumps on racetracks, BMXers figured they might as well practice—all they needed was a mound of dirt, a drop-off, a curb, a loose plank, or a piece of plywood. The only other necessary ingredient was speed, and that was just a matter of sprinting through a lead-in or setting the jump at the bottom of a hill.

RIGHT: Rick Thorne transitions into a one-handed air at the X Games. It only looks out of control.

Ryan Nyquist pulls a tabletop with a busdriver bar spin.

Jay Miron works the lip for an X Games crowd.

Vert's Ups and Downs

In addition to being rooted in motocross, vert riding can also be traced back to the early days of flatland. When the freestyle world was young, flatlanders did their thing in the air as well as on the ground, and when the American Freestyle Association (AFA) was developing, vert and skatepark contests were part of the mix. The contests were held on a quarter-pipe—a curved plywood ramp that riders sprinted toward and followed straight up into the air,

dropping back to earth. Needless to say, these early ramps were less safe, with much more rudimentary transitions—the curved area between the vertical and horizontal portions—than today's ramps.

As was the case with all BMX disciplines, vert started with kids trying to create adventure and avoid boredom. Steve Swope, chief operating officer for Hoffman Bikes and an early vert rider, believes access and culture were also crucial to the sport's roots. "If you had a 20-inch bike, and

there wasn't a track around the corner, you could do it," he recalls. "There were no real rules, and you could do what you wanted. It created its own culture. You have three friends, and it creates a group. You had personalities driven to that who were ready for something new."

In the early 1980s, Swope and his buddies, including vert pioneer Mat Hoffman, were just cruising around their hometown of Edmonds, Oklahoma, riding together after school and finding things to do in empty lots. The local bike shop provided inspiration. Between the stickers, the cool parts, the magazines, and an owner who encouraged people to push their limits, it was hard not to be jazzed just stepping inside the sanctuary.

Swope started out in the sport as the typical BMX kid. Looking for something that was a little crazy and wanting

This is a solid front end: U-brake, gusseted frame joint, four-bolt stem.

RIGHT: This rig and gear might look set up for racing a the ABA Grand Nationals, but T.J. Lavin, one of the world's top dirt jumpers, is seriously boing out this trick. Check out the extension of his legs.

ABOVE: Todd Lyons appears moments from wang-chunging at the ABA Grand Nationals. Still, he's doing an admirable job of trying to recover from the errors of his ways.

to emulate his oldest brother, he first got into motocross. But it was his older brother's chrome Skyway bike that hooked him on BMX. The bike moved him in a way that nothing else had. Then, Hoffman and his brothers saw an ad in the back of *BMX Action* and ordered plans for a quarter-pipe ramp. Their father and uncle built it, and their future was launched. Mat's autobiography, *The Ride of My Life*, tells the whole story.

While the ads for ramp plans can still be found in the back of some BMX mags, most plans have migrated to the Web. And, since most of the people posting the information want to get the word out, most of these plans are free.

Hoffman and his buddies formed the Edmonds Bike Shop Trick Team and put on demonstrations. Just as the team was gaining local notoriety, freestyle began to appear

Mat Hoffman, "The Condor" himself, warms up the crowd with some no-handed air.

on television. The team scored a corporate sponsorship, which lead to more competitions, greater notoriety, and Skyway finally taking aboard Hoffman as a salaried team member.

Vert was exploding. Teams were traveling the country, pulling up to bike shop parking lots, and putting on shows. It was big enough that the AFA decided to hold a major

LEFT: Flipping at the X Games. The rider will land upright.

competition in New York City's Madison Square Garden in 1987. A second group even formed to promote events to rival the AFA. Ron Wilkerson started putting on King of Vert (KoV) and Meet the Street contests. One of the twists on the AFA thing was that he used half-pipes instead of quarters. Another is that Wilkerson's events were rider-organized and run by volunteers.

Then, just as quickly as vert went into giant mode, it burned out. No sponsorship, no tours, nothing. Riders went without rides. Swope believes that by 1991 there were

FAR RIGHT: Hoffman goes off the rack with San Francisco's Golden Gate Bridge as a backdrop.

RIGHT: John Povah gets in some backyard ramp riding. When the apex of flight has been reached, the rider begins looking ahead to re-entry.

BELOW: Dave Mirra flies some one-handed air. This might not be the most thrilling maneuver, but it is only one part of a routine.

less than 10 professional vert riders left in all the United States, but even though the show end of the sport had disappeared, riders kept on doing their thing. Someday, it would rise again.

From out of those ashes rode Hoffman. In 1989, at the age of 17, a high-school dropout and newly unemployed after having made mad cash, Hoffman still wanted to make a living riding his bike and shooting for the sky. He created his own vert team, the Sprocket Jockeys, bought an 18-wheeler, had a large portable half-pipe built, and hit the road. Talk about taking it to the people—the

continued on page 65

A Phoenix local at the annual Burning Bike Festival does his best E.T.

LEFT: Dave Osato, at the apex of air, eyeballs the transition as he prepares to direct his bike back to earth.

Sprocket Jockeys hit all manners of outdoor fairs around the country. There was little glitz and only a bit more money, but it was a job, a mission, a dream. The Sprocket Jockeys rode their bikes and lived their passion to earn their daily bread. If they ground it out long enough, something good would come of it. Today, the list of Jockeys reads like a who's who of vert: Dennis McCoy, Jay Miron, Dave Mirra, and, of course, Hoffman.

The traveling show evolved into the Bicycle Stunt (BS) Series. BS was an update of the contests of the 1980s with a new vibe, one Swope describes as, "Let's make it as true to what the sport is." BS got off the ground in 1992 with six events. It was a call to the BMX trick tribe. Vert, street, park—everyone could come out and play. As BS grew, it came to be considered part of the "extreme sport" wave.

ESPN saw a trend and decided to jump on it. They created the Extreme Games and sponsored the first installment in Providence, Rhode Island, in 1995. The bike portion was organized by the Hoffman Bicycle Association. Naturally, the events got some prime airtime. They were also a super live attraction, drawing almost 200,000 spectators over the course of eight days. It was great for the network and even better for BMX. Trick riding was back and badder than ever. The riding was hot, and it appealed to more than diehard riders—the spectacle enticed the public at large, some of whom were dazzled by the possibilities and decided to try riding.

The Extreme Games were such a success ESPN changed them to the X Games and created a brand name. Vert grew with the X Games, as did dirt jumping and street riding. It was a great association for bikers. The world no longer had to buy videos or magazines to find out about the vibe. Now, they simply had to turn on their televisions.

NBC did trick riding a huge favor by following ESPN's lead and creating the Gravity Games. They started in 1999, also in Providence, Rhode Island. "NBC was looking to fill a void on network TV for programming, and particularly sports programming, that reached the elusive young male

There can be little confusion as to how the Superman seat grab got its moniker.

LEFT: Biff! When a rider completely cases a jump, the coccyx takes the bitter pill.

NEXT: Locals Jerry Badders, Cory Nastazio, and Revel Erickson conduct a skull session in Huntington Beach. When you aren't riding, talking about riding the next best thing.

Cory Nastazio goes can-can while breeching the canyon during a dirt-jump session.

RIGHT: Nastazio…flipping out.

market," explains Joanie McCaw, who worked on the Gravity Games for NBC. They included the same events as the X Games and, like the X Games, worked with the athletes to create a format that appealed to the riders.

Television made vert big time and created celebrities out of guys who went from the pages of specialty magazines to the subjects of international media attention. Funny how a casual thing morphs into a monster.

Vert Bikes

To survive the rigors of vert riding, the bicycles had to change. Air pushed regular components past their breaking points. Conventional wheels couldn't hold up, so manufacturers came out with wheels with extra spokes. Skyway introduced the Tuff Wheel wheel set, which was heavier than wire-spoke wheel sets but almost indestructible. Pegs, rotors ... all the freestyle stuff was also part of the vert package. However, as guys like Mat Hoffman continued to push the envelope of possibility, they started breaking frames monthly, weekly, and sometimes daily. A tougher bike had to be built.

When he sensed that his sponsor wasn't willing to build bikes to meet his needs, Hoffman worked on creating his own bike and company. And while he wasn't the first guy who walked away from factory sponsorship to create his own bike company, he was one of the biggest to do so. He started by working with BMX pioneers Linn Kasten, formerly of Redline, and Mike Devitt of SE Racing. They advised Hoffman and built his first frames. Hoffman Bikes was off the ground.

Rider-run and rider-owned companies have an important place in the development of gear. These were the guys pushing their equipment past the breaking point—they thought they knew how to make it better, and they went for it. The fact that pioneering, rider-founded firms like Redline, GT, and Haro have all become corporate entities says something about BMX.

That said, there's nothing too sophisticated about vert bikes. Obviously, they have to be strong, so their frame tubes are almost always made of 4130 straight-gauge chro-moly. Over time, their components have been built up, refined, and slimmed. U-brakes are hidden inside the stays. The cranks are brawny. The seat is out of the way. The pegs are solid. A good bike is in the 35-pound range. And for all the talk of equipment, the best bike is the one that doesn't get noticed. It's the one that does what the rider wants, when the rider wants, and doesn't fail under pressure.

Dirt Jumping

Like all strains of BMX, dirt jumping goes back to the beginning. Both racetracks and trails had dirt jumps, and practicing takeoffs and landings—maximizing airtime— proved a fine way to spend an afternoon. Love, fun, and the discipline to tackle a scary task are all part of BMX.

Tim "Fuzzy" Hall, a dirt-jumping legend, ties jumping back to the film *On Any Sunday*. "BMX began with dirt jumping, just kind of emulating motocross dudes from *On Any Sunday*," he said. "They just took their Sting-Rays out and started doing it." Some call Hall the Godfather of Dirt Jumping, a moniker he attributes to the fact that he was around before dirt jumping was its own thing.

In most places, trail riding became a good way for riders inspired by *On Any Sunday* to start jumping. Usually, a gnarly crash or two would let the riders know if a jump was poorly designed or too difficult.

As an organized event, dirt jumping got its start with the ABA in the late 1980s, which put on contests at some of its bigger racing events. It was a way for the racers to show off skills other than speed. Hall was racing at the time and slowly moved his way into dirt jumping as it grew.

Also catching that growth curve was Goldie Leshaun Butler, another early dirt jumper who got his start in racing. Goldie started like everyone else, just tooling around town with friends, but became interested in racing and started riding the track at his local YMCA in Orange County, Cali-

fornia. "I was just pedaling around with a couple of friends that I knew," Goldie said. "We pedaled around town, and we looked for spots to ride our bikes at, whether it be going down steep hills or looking for stuff to jump off of. Anything, as long as we had our bikes with us. It was fun."

As Butler was working his way up to a pro-class racer, he saw jumping coming on the scene. "They started holding jumping contests on the tracks at some of these nationals," he recalled. "I was just watching. There was Dennis McCoy and Dave Mirra, Chris Moeller, and Mike Griffin. They were freestyle guys; they didn't really race. I can't leave out the fact that Fuzzy and Brian Foster were the bigger influences to me, because they raced *and* they jumped."

Both Goldie and Fuzzy were aided in their shift to dirt jumping by the mania that the X Games created. Fuzzy first saw the sport going legit in 1996 and 1997, when regular contests appeared.

Dirt-jumping contests are not dissimilar to mogul skiing contests—gravity gained on a downward slope gives the rider enough speed to take the first jump, then the rest of the jumps on a run are based on the momentum gained from the first. "It's judged on the tricks you do," Hall explains. "You have three or four runs and drop your worst run. Anywhere from 10 seconds to 20 seconds."

Fuzzy and Goldie both excel at contest riding, but it's the everyday stuff that makes riding special for them. Fuzzy might have a video game and a bike line named after him, but trail riding and jumping in his backyard are what are really special to him. He has converted the property behind his house into a dirt-jumping nirvana. Like the sport itself, the yard is all about evolution, and it is constantly being refined.

Fuzzy's yard is the result of years of expertise. Newbies can read their way to building jumps on the Internet, where a number of sites have detailed instructions and photographs about creating perfect jumps.

Goldie finds heading down the road to tackle both the familiar and the unknown the thing that makes riding

The other side of flipping out. Joe Rich is failing and falling. Only his outstretched arms will save him from lawn darting.

important. "It's kind of like a meditation for me. It's a total way of exercise, a feeling of oneness with you and your bike, and just almost like a constant, colorful slideshow where you have different surroundings, and you're able to feel differently at each place," he explains. "It's fun when you can pedal fast down the road and check out life. It helps me clear my mind and focus on the positivity of life."

Goldie thinks the best way to get involved is to follow your interests. "If you have dirt, then build a jump. If you have concrete, then you work with that. If you have only a parking lot, learn how to ride flatland. Learn how to do 180s and roll backwards. Use what you have, and that forms what kind of rider you'll be."

Dirt-Jump Bikes

Dirt-jump bikes don't have to be as robust as their vert brethren, as they are ridden on slightly more forgiving terrain. Fuzzy stresses 4130 chro-moly as the key. Goldie agrees, and says that aluminum frames can't handle the stress of jumping. His only requirements for a dirt-jump bike are a Gyro and pegs. Fuzzy likes the feeling of having the bars pulled back. No matter what you do, so long as the bike can take a pounding and is comfortable, it's ready for riding.

The X-up is a classic maneuver, dating back to the earliest days of BMX racing.

chapter 4

STREET/PARK
bmx begins & ends in the street

A Phoenix Arizona local grinds a rail as his buddy gets it all on video.
Grinding a railing is definitely smoother than taking the steps.

"Everything begins with the street," says Rob "Smartbomb" Smart. "There's a street out your door. You have to take that street to get anywhere, and you have to take that street home." The former pro and current president of Smart-bomb Entertainment ties street riding to the roots of BMX. It's a valuable point—street is essential to riding.

Yes, everyone rides in the street, but whether or not you treat it as a playground is another story. In many respects, street is about environment, using what's available, what's nearby, and what's already built. These attributes make street riding the most economical and, in many ways, the most natural of all BMX disciplines. All you need is a bike and a direction.

"Street" is riding your bike and finding things to do wherever you go. Can a set of stairs be cleaned? What about grinding the railing? Maybe try using that drop-off as a launch point for a 360. It helps to have like-minded friends who are ready to try anything and are willing to share their knowledge. When buddies get together, riding becomes a social, physical, and spiritual experience. The point is to have fun, but developing skills and personal growth often come along with it.

Van Homan, one of today's top dogs of street, says street is simple. "You ride around with buddies. There are streets everywhere. You don't need a ramp, you don't need a jump, you just ride it." For Homan, it's a way of life. "You're just out there, finding things. You'll just have an idea in your mind, a concept that you want to try, and you search the world looking for it. For a certain ledge, it's worth going across the world."

People have been riding street for as long as there's been BMX. Street became its own thing in 1987 when Ron Wilkerson started Meet the Street contests. Wilkerson remembers, "It was in Lakeside, California, outside of San Diego. It was in a parking lot with a banked wall. We just set up a bunch of ramps and a car and did the first street contest."

Wilkerson and his friends wanted the contest to resemble the riding they did every day. "We'd just go out

Old school fence ride, Woodland Hills, California. The hair-metal hightops expose the fact it's 1988.

LEFT: Jamming during a night session. Besides the stealth nature of night riding, there is a spooky and surreal calm that goes with the night.

A street rider bunnyhops down a set of stairs in Phoenix, Arizona. The bunnyhop is one of the most elemental moves in all BMX disciplines.

and ride and find stuff to do. The only contests of the time were quarter-pipe tricks and flatland. We wanted to make a contest that reflected our type of riding." It was a roots movement, a way to get back to the basics of riding, with friends and acquaintances hanging out, jamming, trying to show off to one another—the stuff that makes riding fun.

At a certain level, there is something ironic about creating a street contest. At face value, it seems inorganic, but if people are going to do something, they're bound to get competitive, and that's where contests figure in. That first Meet the Street contest in 1987 offered $1,000 in prize money. It was a motivation, an excuse to train, to compete for those bragging rights.

Thanks to the X Games, the Gravity Games, and the like, street contests are big today—lucrative, televised, and popular the world over. Mat Hoffman is still in the sport on the promotion end with his Crazy Freakin' Bikers events. Fun can be serious business.

Despite the serious business side, street can still be fun. Even competitive riders ride for fun in their spare time; that's their training. Pros get as good as they are because they find riding to be irresistible fun, a thirst they can never quench.

"You get your bikes in the shop, you beg your parents for a bike, you start in the street. Then, they migrate to dirt, plywood ramps, racing, dirt, or a skatepark," Rob

Phoenix-area local "Rat Boy" rides a wall in a wash. Work with what you have—creativity will ensue.

A fisheye lens makes the confusing even more so. With the Pacific Ocean in the background, this rider has broken the bonds with earth to ride a wall in Huntington Beach.

PREVIOUS: The wall stall—don't overshoot and be ready for the return to the terra firma.

That's photographer Tony Donaldson taking his race setup, his Chucks, his Dr. J shorts, and his mullet to the street back in '89.

Smart explains. "It's the love, it's what you love to do. It's when you're playing baseball and thinking about riding your bike." That's when you know you're hooked. Mat Hoffman, Goldie Leshaun Butler, and all of today's greats played the sports that their parents and their friends found worthwhile, but the gravitational pull of the bike drew them away from those activities.

Street can be imposing. There are no rules, no code, no printed matter with rules on advancing. Often, the sport just looks like a bunch of people slowly riding around, but then you find out that those guys who look like they're doing nothing are pulling off some amazing things when no one is looking—things that are usually seen only on TV. The fact that street is largely undefined shows how free it can be. See a bunch of guys hanging around, pulling moves you never thought possible? How do you break into that?

Everyone has to start small. Homan knows that the big tricks don't happen on the first day. "You start out doing small ledges, you learn simple things. You learn how to bunnyhop higher. It's just progression. It's like anything. You definitely try to ride when there aren't a lot of people around. People don't want you riding on their property. It makes them nervous. They're worried that you're going to sue."

And Homan says you shouldn't worry what other riders think. "I think that one thing I've liked about street, it's not as competitive. It's more on your own terms. It's more your own progression, your own goals. I just enjoy that." Learn from others, enjoy their successes, learn from their failures, and try to impress yourself.

"It's a dream process, you dream about it," says Smart, who sees himself as a BMX lifer and believes that anyone's development as a rider depends on imagining the next thing, the next trick, seeing a way to link two moves together. "You dream them in your sleep at night, you daydream at school. You take something to the next level. Bicycle riding is not really a thought pattern—riding your bike is a feeling. Your bike becomes one with you. The guy who rides his bike the most is going to be the best."

Taking a tailwhip in the air. This is a classic flatland stunt adapted for ramp and park riding.

At skateparks, about the only things more common than feeble grinds—rear peg on the coping, front wheel on the deck—are skid lids.

For many kids, street riding is a form of personal expression, a way to grab control of one's life, to get places without the help of parents or sitters. Riding takes you far from the rigid patterns that often form in school and at home. It can be intoxicating, and it's something that even a lifer can feel fresh about. "When you're a child, you want a little anarchy, you want to rebel," says Smart. Looking to do things that are a bit unusual, maybe even slightly dangerous, is a classic desire and one that street can easily quench.

Rider Preference

In street riding, aesthetic transcends design. The bike has to *feel* right, and part of that is in the setup. It takes a short frame with upright angles and pegs, but whether the bars are tilted forward or back, whether there are two sets of pegs or one, whether or not there's a sprocket-guard to protect the chainrings is all about rider preference. Homan, who doesn't use a sprocket-guard, explained that rider preference extends to cranks as well. "You can get big, beefy cranks, which will last forever, or you can run something lighter that won't last as long."

Wheels are also a component that can be dictated by one's riding style. Homan uses 36-spoked wheels in front and 48 in back. Some riders go with 48 front and rear, while gentler riders might prefer 36 front and rear.

Homan does see a few guidelines, however. "There are definitely bikes that are better for street. You need something with strong dropouts. You want 4310 chro-moly. It's good to find a happy medium between light and strong. It can only be so light."

Riding street is very much like going without a rope. Shorts and a T-shirt might be comfortable, but that isn't the wisest selection of riding gear. And as with all BMX disciplines, a good flat sneaker is best. Pants are also part of the uniform, with pads underneath. More experienced riders go with lighter pads, while the less experienced go with more. "Any pads are good, [they] are going to save you," Homan said. "When I ride street, [I wear] just knee gaskets, a thin knee pad under my pants. I don't like elbow pads. I usually don't ride with a helmet [when] riding street. You're just cruising around, or hanging out."

Of course, Homan's a pro with years of experience. Fresh-faced newcomers should consider more protection, including a helmet.

RIGHT: It feels better when you have an audience. A rider executes a railslide for an X Games crowd.

Ryan Nyquist goes way beyond the lip on this wallride at the 2000 Beach Bash in Hermosa Beach, California.

Park Riding

Park (or skatepark) riding has been around for almost 30 years and is just slightly newer than BMX itself. The skatepark concept first came around when skateboarders started riding around in empty pools, which most agree started some time after skateboard wheels were revolutionized in the early 1970s. There's some disagreement as to whether the first skatepark was built in Florida or in California, but it *was* built sometime between 1974 and 1976.

It was probably a public facility, and it probably had cement bowls that could be ridden by both bikers and skaters.

Parks have many benefits over streets. They're closed off from cars, pedestrians, and dogs. They're designed to be ridden. They offer controlled challenges. On the whole, skateparks are great places for a beginner and great for minimizing thinking. Park designers determine what riders can safely accomplish and then build parks to meet those possibilities.

Mike Daly, a rider and park designer, thinks parks can create perfect riding environments: "The skatepark has some of the elements that can be found in the street, but exaggerated so that they are perfect for riding. Plus, there is some stuff you are never going to find in the street." This makes the riding more predictable and safer, and makes for a great environment to start out in.

As skateparks grew in popularity, different types were developed. Private parks, which can be indoors or out, usually comprise a series of plywood ramps of differing sizes.

Private parks have more supervision as well as limitations on riding time, and many offer classes for those who want to learn from an expert. Some private parks also have foam pits, which make attempting jumps easier.

More often than not, public parks are made of poured cement and are almost always outside. While there might be someone minding the door, the park itself is for the most part unsupervised, and the bikers and skaters usually mingle.

Bob Haro, R.L. Osborn, and the early freestyle crowd rode parks. It was just part of the game. Bob Morales rec-

Nyquist appears suspended in midair and sporting his trademark backtrail bar spin.

ognized this when he included King of the Skateparks as a facet of his American Freestyle Association (AFA) contests. In the early days of the AFA, Eddie Fiola was the champ. Morales dubbed him "King of the Skateparks," and the name stuck. Angie "sKwirl" McEwen of www.notfreestylin.com refers to Fiola as "preschool," as in preceding old school. In Fiola's day, the AFA combined ramp riding, flatland, and park into one competition, so participants had to do everything well to excel. The early vert and freestyle riders were also good at park, and that made the sport fun; each group had its own strengths and weaknesses but was flexible enough to try anything. Fiola, the stunt double star of *Rad* and now a Hollywood stuntman, liked the early days. "I don't see myself as just ramps or just ground. It's everything."

Skateparks had faddish excitement going for them in the 1980s. Crazy new sports with improbable stunts were appealing but not big enough to survive the wave that came crashing down as the fad lost steam. Many, if not most, skateparks closed down towards the end of that decade. Maybe there were fewer kids riding, but regardless, people weren't buying enough bikes and skateboards to keep the facilities open.

One top park rider rode though the cold, dark days of winter—and through the winter of park riding—indoors. Taj Mihelich, of Terrible One Bikes, grew up in Michigan. "We were looking for a place inside to ride. They were very scarce back then," Taj remembered. "There was a little one [locally], but the main [one] was in Chicago, a six-hour drive away." The "little one" was good enough for practicing. Taj hit his first comp in 1991 in Iowa at an indoor park that was an eight-hour drive from home.

The scenes at the comps in those days weren't one of the bright lights, big-city happenings that they are today.

When they tell you the X Games are a grind, this is what they mean.

"Back then, it was only riders," Taj explains. "You just tried stuff you never tried before. Everyone was just trying their own thing and going for it."

Rob Smart thinks that BMX lives and dies in seven-year cycles that are influenced by many factors. The bottom of the biggest BMX bust was in the early 1990s. Park riding—like racing, vert, and street—picked up after that point. It, too, benefited from the X Games, Gravity Games, and Crazy Freakin' Bikers events.

Mark Losey, a staffer at *Ride BMX* magazine believes this is a hot time for parks. "Just about everywhere is getting a cement, publicly funded outdoor park," he says. "There are tons of private indoor pay parks." Currently, there are over 1,000 public parks in the United States, with another 1,000 in the works. There are anywhere between 300 and 500 private parks. Taj sees some regional differences in the park scene. "In the Northwest, there's a ton of public cement parks. On the East Coast, there are more indoor, private wood parks," he says. He thinks some of the regional differences have to do with local laws, but it could just as easily have to do with active bike shops and parents looking for safe outlets for their kids.

Despite the growth of the park world, all is not well—BMX bikes have become *machina non grata* at many parks. It's the classic user dispute that flares up wherever there are slightly competing interests. Since "skate" is the first part of skateparks, many assume that the parks are for skaters only. As a result, many parks, both public and private, have limited or even banned bikes from riding. It's an ironic development, as most of those old enough to have experienced the preschool and old-school days of BMX remember the trouble skaters routinely got in, and how skaters popularized the slogan, "Skateboarding is not a crime."

Three organizations are trying to combat the problem: Skatepark Association USA, BMX Riders Organization, and Access BMX. Mark is one of the founders of Access BMX, which compiles a fairly comprehensive list of parks that are open to riding and the details therein.

It's hard to say where the skater–biker conflict came from. Bikers don't think it's them. They think that some hardcore skaters were there first and influenced the thinking of the various powers that be. Mark thinks everyone can easily get along. "All together is fine with us. Bikers and skaters can get along fine in parks," he says. "As long as you're heads-up while riding, it should be okay. One of the most important things is not to throw off a vibe of 'I'm a biker.' You're all there for the same thing. When you're not riding, you want to make sure to stay out of the way."

Taj is concerned about the negatives that skaters see. "There are more sharp things on a bike that can damage a park," he admits. "It's really easy to buy caps for the end of your pegs or pegs with softer ends. It's just using common sense, being courteous, not throwing your bike when you crash. There's an unwritten code of etiquette. Wait your turn. Don't drop in the way."

Mark believes each park has its own rules and standards of etiquette. "When starting out, go to the park during a mellow session," he advises.

Whereas street riding is so free as to be imposing, unwritten rules and a site full of people who seem to know what they're doing can be equally daunting. Taj recommends laying low and observing before starting in a park. "Watch first, see where everyone is going, find where the lines are, and don't get in others' way—give others in the park respect."

Starting out in park riding has its own difficulties. The first move is the hardest. It's a good idea to read up in magazines and watch videos—there are even some how-to's—before ramping it up in a park. Of course, some things can always be practiced at home. You want to be comfortable with the bike before going to a park. Ride it around, jump curbs and try wheelies, endos, whatever you can do to gain confidence and understand how to control the bike in all situations. In addition to the classes offered at some parks, there are even summer camps that focus on park riding. Although there is also the fear factor

Pat Miller pulls a no-hander, no-footer while riding an indoor SoCal park. Pads should be a part of any BMX uniform, though leopard print is optional.

LEFT: Ryan Nyquist nails the nothing can-can while riding at his home in Greenville, North Carolina.

of looking stupid, remember that all experienced riders have the same response: If you show up and try hard, people will respect you.

One other thing: Crashing is inevitable. The best thing is to be prepared to go down. Gear starts with a helmet. The stylin' way to go is with a skateboard helmet, but the most experienced riders believe that for neophytes, a full-face helmet makes a lot of sense. Elbow and knee pads are also essential for starting out. The ones that have hard caps—firm plastic on the outside—are a good choice, as they protect well and allow the wearer a chance to slide to safety on them. Hoffman, McNeil, and others offer variations on park pegs.

Bikes for the Park

Although the owner of a bike company, Taj Mihelich believes that all bike designs have come so far in the past few years that pretty much anything will do. "The stuff is amazingly standard. Almost any high-end bike would be good," he says. The key is to have smooth tires to better grip the surfaces. And, as with any BMX discipline, one of the most important things is to make sure the bike is in good working condition, no matter what you're riding.

Mark's parting advice on park riding is simple: "Go there to have fun. Don't get intimidated. The park is for everyone."

Finish Line

Reading about the different disciplines of BMX might make them seem like separate cultures. That's only true when one is too keyed in on a single thing. The people who stick at the sport long enough consider themselves riders first. They have a specialty, but they ride whatever they can whenever they can because the riding bug resides deep in their soul. A trick rider, for example, may have an arsenal of moves, but the bike is the link to all enjoyment. Many start out doing one thing in BMX but wind up doing another and another still, all the while finding their first love in the sport interesting and worthwhile.

Smartbomb, the BMX lifer whose roots go so far back he was at the first Meet the Street event, spends a fair amount of time talking about how important it is to love all of the sport's disciplines and to do the sport for that reason alone. He thinks everyone would be better off if they took a more holistic approach to riding. "I think that everybody should do what they feel in their heart, but it would be better for the sport and the athlete if they would entertain the idea of being the best at every element at BMX," Smartbomb says. "It would make them a better athlete. It would open their mind to positive experiences."

Ride.

Nyquist executes a flip on an indoor ramp.

author bios

J.P. PARTLAND

J. P. Partland first swung a leg over a bicycle when he was three. Little did he know it would become a lifelong obsession. An avid cyclist, his work has appeared on numerous Web sites and in more than 50 cycling-specific and general-interest magazines, including *Velo News, Bicycling, Bicyclist, Bike,* and *Outside*. In addition to his work as a journalist, he has performed stand-up comedy and written plays, teleplays, and short stories. He finds there is never enough time to ride and never enough room for bikes. The author of MBI's *Mountain Bike Madness*, Partland lives in New York City.

tony donaldson

Less than nine months after shooting his first photograph, Tony Donaldson moved 2,000 miles to work on staff at one of his favorite magazines. Although he's had no formal training, his photography has since appreared in the likes of *ESPN the Magazine* and *Sports Illustrated for Kids*, and in print advertisements for several top shoe, clothing, and bicycle companies. An avid mountain biker, BMXer, and skateboarder, Donaldson also works in the realm of digital video-making, editing, and postproduction. He lives in the Los Angeles area, and his work can be viewed at www. tdphoto.com.

Other MBI Publishing Company titles of interest:

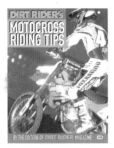

**Dirt Rider's
Motocross Riding Tips**
ISBN 0-7603-1315-6

**Lines: The Snowboard
Photography of Sean Sullivan**
ISBN 0-7603-1678-3

**Freeestyle Motocross II:
Air Sickness**
ISBN 0-7603-1184-6

Mountain Bike Madness
ISBN 0-7603-1440-3

Streetbike Extreme
ISBN 0-7603-1299-0

Schwinn
ISBN 1-58068-003-8

The Cars of Gran Turismo
ISBN 0-7603-1495-0

Sport Compacts
ISBN 0-7603-1496-9

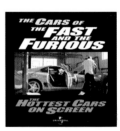

**The Cars of
The Fast and the Furious**
ISBN 0-7603-1551-5

Find us on the Internet at www.motorbooks.com 1-800-826-6600